I0415790

March 2012

DOD FINANCIAL MANAGEMENT

The Army Faces Significant Challenges in Achieving Audit Readiness for Its Military Pay

GAO

Accountability ★ Integrity ★ Reliability

G A O

Accountability * Integrity * Reliability

Highlights

Highlights of GAO-12-406, a report to congressional committees

DOD FINANCIAL MANAGEMENT

The Army Faces Significant Challenges in Achieving Audit Readiness for Its Military Pay

Why GAO Did This Study

The Defense Finance and Accounting Service-Indianapolis (DFAS-IN) reported that fiscal year 2010 active Army military payroll totaled $46.1 billion. However, for several years, GAO and others have reported continuing deficiencies with Army military payroll processes and controls, raising questions about the validity and accuracy of reported Army military pay and whether it is auditable. The Department of Defense (DOD) has recently accelerated its Statement of Budgetary Resources audit readiness goal by 3 months to 2014 and is required to achieve audit readiness for a full set of DOD financial statements by 2017. GAO performed basic audit procedures for the Army's active duty military payroll to assess the Army's ability to (1) identify a valid population of payroll transactions and (2) test a sample of payroll transactions for validity and accuracy. GAO reviewed applicable laws and regulations, analyzed DOD and Army policies and procedures, drew a statistical sample of payroll transactions to test their accuracy and validity, and met with DOD, DFAS-IN, Army, and Defense Manpower Data Center officials.

What GAO Recommends

GAO is making four recommendations to help the Army develop the processes and controls necessary to achieve financial statement audit readiness, including identifying and validating the population of military payroll transactions and obtaining and retaining necessary pay-affecting documents. The Army concurred with GAO's four recommendations and noted actions it is taking.

View GAO-12-406. For more information, contact Asif A. Khan at (202) 512-9869 or khana@gao.gov.

What GAO Found

The Army could not readily identify the population of Army military payroll accounts given its existing procedures and systems. The Army and DFAS-IN did not have an effective, repeatable process for identifying the population of active duty payroll records. For example, it took 3 months and repeated attempts before DFAS-IN could provide a population of service members who received active duty Army military pay in fiscal year 2010. Further, because the Army does not have an integrated military personnel and payroll system, it was necessary to compare the payroll file to active Army personnel records. However, the Defense Manpower Data Center (DMDC), DOD's central repository for information on DOD-affiliated personnel, did not have an effective process for comparing military pay account files with military personnel files to identify a valid population of military payroll transactions. It took DMDC over 2 months and labor-intensive research to compare and reconcile the total number of fiscal year 2010 active duty payroll accounts to its database of personnel files. DOD's *Financial Improvement and Audit Readiness (FIAR) Guidance* states that identifying the population of transactions is a key task essential to achieving audit readiness. Without effective processes for identifying the population of Army military pay records and comparing military pay accounts to personnel records, the Army will have difficulty meeting DOD's 2014 audit readiness goal for the Statement of Budgetary Resources.

In addition, the Army does not have an efficient or effective process or system for providing supporting documents for Army military payroll. For example, DFAS-IN had difficulty retrieving and providing usable Leave and Earnings Statement files and the Army was unable to locate or provide supporting personnel documents for GAO's statistical sample of fiscal year 2010 Army military pay accounts. GAO's *Standards for Internal Control in the Federal Government* and DOD's FIAR Guidance provide that audited entities document transactions and events and assure that supporting documentation can be identified, located, and provided for examination. Although the Army deployed the Interactive Personnel Management System (iPERMS) as the Army's Official Military Personnel File in 2007, it had not consistently or completely populated iPERMS with personnel records. At the end of September 2011, 6 months after receiving GAO's 250 statistical sample items, the Army and DFAS-IN were able to provide complete documentation for 2 of GAO's sample items and provided partial documentation for 3 items, but provided no documentation for 245 of GAO's 250 sample items.

The Army has begun several military pay audit readiness efforts that, if successfully implemented, could help increase the likelihood of meeting DOD's 2014 Statement of Budgetary Resources audit readiness goal and the 2017 mandate for audit readiness on a complete set of DOD financial statements. These efforts include documenting and testing payroll system application controls, documenting Army military pay business processes, identifying the range of supporting documents for military pay, and developing an integrated military personnel and payroll system. Most of these efforts are not yet documented and, therefore, there is no assurance that they will be implemented timely and effectively.

_____ **United States Government Accountability Office**

Contents

Letter		1
	Background	5
	Process and System Weaknesses Hindered Army's Ability to Identify a Valid Population of Military Payroll Transactions	12
	The Army Was Unable to Provide Documentation to Support the Validity and Accuracy of a Sample of Payroll Transactions	16
	Conclusions	26
	Recommendations for Executive Action	27
	Agency Comments and Our Evaluation	28

Appendix I	Objectives, Scope, and Methodology	31

Appendix II	Comments from the Department of the Army	35

Appendix III	GAO Contact and Staff Acknowledgments	38

Figures		
	Figure 1: Army Process for Creating a Military Pay Record for an Enlisted Service Member	8
	Figure 2: Overview of Major Systems Involved in Processing Active Army Military Payroll	11
	Figure 3: Test Results for 5 of 250 Soldier Pay Account Sample Items	21

Abbreviations

ARISS	Army Recruiting Information Support System
ASA (M&RA)	Assistant Secretary of the Army for Manpower and Reserve Affairs
COBOL	Common Business Oriented Language
CFO	Chief Financial Officer
CIGIE	Council of the Inspectors General on Integrity and Efficiency
DA	Department of the Army
DD	Defense Department
DDRS-AFS	Defense Departmental Reporting System–Audited Financial Statements
DDRS-B	Defense Departmental Reporting System–Budgetary
DFAS-IN	Defense Finance and Accounting Service in Indianapolis
DIMHRS	Defense Integrated Military Human Resource System
DJMS–AC	Defense Joint Military Pay System–Active Component
DMDC	Defense Manpower Data Center
DMPO	Defense Military Pay Office
DOD	Department of Defense
EFT	Electronic funds transfer
FAM	Financial Audit Manual
FIAR	Financial Improvement and Audit Readiness
FIP	Financial Improvement Plan
FISCAM	Federal Information System Controls Audit Manual
FMR	Financial Management Regulation
FSA	Family Separation Allowance
GAAP	Generally Accepted Accounting Principles
GWOT	Global War on Terrorism
HRC	Human Resources Command
iPERMS	Interactive Personnel Management System
IPPS-A	Integrated Personnel and Pay System–Army
MEPS	Military Entrance Processing Station
MPRJ	Military Personnel Records Jacket
Mil Pay Ops	Military Pay Operations
NARA	National Archives and Records Administration
NDAA	National Defense Authorization Act
OMPF	Official Military Personnel File
OUSD(C)	Office of the Under Secretary of Defense (Comptroller) and Chief Financial Officer
PCIE	President's Council on Integrity and Efficiency
PDF	Adobe Portable Document Format

RECBASS	Reception Battalion Automated Support System
SRD-1	Standard Financial System (STANFINS) Redesign Subsystem-1
SSAE	Statements on Standards for Attestation Engagements
SSN	Social Security Number
STANFINS	Standard Financial System
USD (P&R)	Under Secretary of Defense for Personnel and Readiness
USMEPCOM	U.S. Military Entrance Processing Command

United States Government Accountability Office
Washington, DC 20548

March 22, 2012

Congressional Committees

According to the Defense Finance and Accounting Service in Indianapolis (DFAS-IN), fiscal year 2010 active Army military payroll totaled $46.1 billion. For years, we and others have reported continuing deficiencies with Department of the Army military payroll processes and controls. In November 2003, we reported that weaknesses in processes and controls resulted in over- and underpayments to mobilized Army National Guard personnel.[1] In April 2006, we reported that pay problems rooted in complex, cumbersome processes used to pay Army soldiers from initial mobilization through active duty deployment to demobilization resulted in military debt to battle-injured soldiers.[2] In June 2009, we reported that the Army did not have effective controls for processing and accounting for military personnel federal payroll taxes because of weaknesses in its procedures and controls for assuring accurate and timely documentation of transactions.[3] In July 2011, the Department of Defense (DOD) Inspector General reported that the Defense Finance and Accounting Service (DFAS)[4] made potentially invalid active duty military payroll payments of $4.2 million from January 2005 through December 2009 for the Army, the Navy, and the Air Force.[5]

These reported continuing deficiencies in Army payroll processes and controls have called into question the extent to which the Army's military

---

[1]GAO, *Military Pay: Army National Guard Personnel Mobilized to Active Duty Experienced Significant Pay Problems*, GAO-04-89 (Washington, D.C.: Nov. 13, 2003).

[2]GAO, *Military Pay: Hundreds of Battle-Injured GWOT Soldiers Have Struggled to Resolve Military Debts*, GAO-06-494 (Washington, D.C.: Apr. 27, 2006).

[3]GAO, *Military Pay: The Defense Finance and Accounting Service–Indianapolis Could Improve Control Activities over Its Processing of Active Duty Army Military Personnel Federal Payroll Taxes*, GAO-09-557R (Washington, D.C.: June 18, 2009).

[4]DFAS refers to DFAS-Indianapolis, which processes military pay for the Army and the Air Force, and DFAS-Cleveland, which processes military pay for the Navy and the Marine Corps.

[5]DOD Inspector General, *Active Duty Military Personnel Accounts Were Generally Valid and Secure, but DoD May have Made Improper Payments*, D-2011-093 (Arlington, VA: July 27, 2011).

payroll transactions are valid and accurate and whether the Army's military payroll as a whole is auditable. The Army's military pay is material to all of the Army's financial statements and comprises about 20 percent of the Army's $233.8 billion in reported fiscal year 2010 net outlays.[6] Accordingly, Army active duty military payroll is significant to both Army and DOD efforts to meet DOD's 2014 Statement of Budgetary Resources audit readiness goal.

The Chief Financial Officers Act of 1990, as amended, established requirements for 24 agencies, including DOD, to prepare annual financial statements and have them audited.[7] As we have previously reported, DOD's many challenges in resolving its pervasive and long-standing weaknesses in financial management, business operations, and systems have inhibited its ability to meet this requirement.[8] DOD has undertaken numerous financial management improvement initiatives over the years, but it continues to receive disclaimers of opinion on its financial statements.

The National Defense Authorization Act (NDAA) for Fiscal Year 2010 mandated that DOD be prepared to validate (certify) that its consolidated financial statements are ready for audit by September 30, 2017.[9] The NDAA for fiscal year 2010 also mandated that DOD develop and maintain a Financial Improvement and Audit Readiness (FIAR) Plan that includes, among other things, the specific actions to be taken and costs associated with correcting the financial management deficiencies that impair the department's ability to prepare timely, reliable, and complete financial

---

[6]Outlays during a fiscal year may be for payment of obligations incurred in prior years or in the same year. Net outlays are disbursements net of offsetting collections.

[7]Pub. L. No. 101-576, § 303, 104 Stat. 2838, 2849, (Nov. 15, 1990), *codified, as amended at* 31 U.S.C. § 3515.

[8]GAO, *DOD Financial Management: Numerous Challenges Must Be Addressed to Improve Auditability,* GAO-11-864T (Washington, D.C.: July 28, 2011); *DOD Financial Management: Numerous Challenges Must Be Addressed to Improve Reliability of Financial Information,* GAO-11-835T (Washington, D.C.: July 27, 2011); and *High-Risk Series: An Update,* GAO-11-278 (Washington, D.C.: February 2011).

[9]Pub. L. No. 111-84, § 1003, 123 Stat. 2190, 2439-40 (Oct. 28, 2009).

management information.[10] Military pay is significant to departmentwide financial statements. Further, other military components, such as the Air Force and the Navy, share some of the same process and system risks as the Army.

In May 2011, the Army reported that it expected to be ready for an audit of its Statement of Budgetary Resources by the first quarter of fiscal year 2015. The Army also reported that its military pay would be audit ready by the first quarter of fiscal year 2015. On October 13, 2011, the Secretary of Defense directed the department to achieve audit readiness for the Statement of Budgetary Resources by the end of fiscal year 2014 as an interim milestone for DOD to meet the legal requirement in the NDAA for Fiscal Year 2010 to achieve full audit readiness for all DOD financial statements by 2017.[11] This new goal would accelerate the time frames for audit readiness of the Army's Statement of Budgetary Resources, including Army military pay, by 3 months. Military pay audit readiness is an important element of this goal.

This report was initiated under our mandate to audit the U.S. government's financial statements.[12] Our objectives were to perform basic audit procedures necessary to conclude about the validity and accuracy of Army's active duty military payroll. Those basic audit procedures included (1) identifying a valid population of military payroll transactions and (2) testing a sample of payroll transactions for validity and accuracy.

To address our first objective, we obtained the population of Army active duty military payroll records from the Defense Finance and Accounting Service, Indianapolis (DFAS-IN). Because the Army does not have an integrated military personnel and payroll system, we worked with the Defense Manpower Data Center (DMDC) (DOD's central source for personnel information) to match DFAS-IN payroll accounts to DMDC

---

[10]The FIAR Plan, which was first prepared in 2005, is DOD's strategic plan and management tool for guiding, monitoring, and reporting on the department's financial management improvement efforts. As such, the plan communicates incremental progress in addressing the department's financial management weaknesses and achieving financial statement auditability.

[11]DOD, Secretary of Defense Memorandum, "Improving Financial Information and Achieving Audit Readiness," October 13, 2011.

[12]31 U.S.C. §§ 331(e), 717(b)(1).

personnel records to determine whether the population of Army military payroll accounts was in agreement with the population of personnel records in DMDC.[13] Nearly all of the identified differences related to service members in separation status. However, we referred six unresolved duplicate items to DMDC and Army Human Resources Command for further research and correction. To address our second objective, we used the population of matched personnel and payroll records to select a statistical sample of 250 soldiers for testing payroll accuracy for the sampled items. We requested 12 months of fiscal year 2010 Leave and Earnings Statements for each soldier in our sample, the most recent data available, to compare pay transactions with supporting Army personnel documents indicating such information as military orders, special duty and expertise entitlements, marital status, and dependent information. We focused on key steps to be followed in establishing military personnel records on specific pay and allowance amounts. We interviewed Army Personnel, Human Resources Command, and Finance Command officials and visited a Military Enlistment Program Station in Indianapolis, Indiana, and a military reception battalion at a training installation at Ft. Jackson, South Carolina, to document the processes for capturing pay-related information and setting up military personnel records. In addition, we interviewed finance officials at Defense Military Pay Offices at two Army field installations to gain an understanding of how pay accounts are established, adjusted, and documented.

We conducted this performance audit from June 2010 through March 2012 in accordance with generally accepted government auditing standards. Those standards require that we plan and perform the audit to obtain sufficient, appropriate evidence to provide a reasonable basis for our findings and conclusions based on our audit objectives. We believe that the evidence obtained provides a reasonable basis for our findings and conclusions based on our audit objectives. Appendix I provides further details on our scope and methodology. Other matters identified in our work that merit management's attention will be reported in a separate letter to Army management.

---

[13]We relied on work performed by DMDC because we reviewed its quality control procedures and found them to be adequate for our audit purposes.

Background

The United States Army is responsible for land-based military operations. It is the largest and oldest established branch of the U.S. military. The modern Army has its roots in the Continental Army, which was formed on June 14, 1775, before the establishment of the United States, to meet the demands of the American Revolutionary War. The Army's mission is to fight and win our nation's wars by providing prompt, sustained land dominance across the full range of military operations and spectrum of conflict in support of combatant commands. The Army does this by organizing, equipping, and training forces; accomplishing missions assigned by the President, the Secretary of Defense, and combatant commanders; and transforming for the future.

For fiscal year 2010, Congress appropriated more than $52 billion to the "Military Personnel, Army" appropriation, which is a 1-year appropriation available for the pay, benefits, incentives, allowances, housing, subsistence, travel, and training primarily for active duty service members.[14] The Defense Finance and Accounting Service in Indianapolis, Indiana (DFAS-IN) is responsible for accounting, disbursement, and reporting for the Army's military personnel costs using the Defense Joint Military Pay System-Active Component (DJMS-AC). According to DFAS-IN, of the $52 billion in fiscal year 2010 military personnel appropriations, the Army's nearly 680,000 service members received $46.1 billion in pay and allowances. To provide payroll support to the vast number of active Army service members, DFAS-IN has over 40 Defense Military Pay Offices within the United States that provide finance services to military personnel in designated geographical areas.

Statement of Budgetary Resources

The Statement of Budgetary Resources is the only financial statement predominantly derived from an entity's budgetary accounts in accordance with budgetary accounting rules, which are incorporated into generally accepted accounting principles (GAAP) for the federal government. The Statement of Budgetary Resources is designed to provide information on authorized budgeted spending authority as reported in the Budget of the United States Government (President's Budget), including budgetary

---

[14]Department of Defense Appropriations Act, 2010, Pub. L. No. 111-118, 123 Stat. 3409, 3410, 3458 (Dec. 19, 2009); Supplemental Appropriations Act, 2010, Pub. L. No. 111-212,124 Stat. 2302, 2305 (July 29, 2010).

resources, availability of budgetary resources, and how budgetary resources have been used.[15]

For fiscal year 2010, the Army reported $331.8 billion in total budgetary resources and over $233.8 billion in net outlays (spending, net of offsetting collections[16]). The Army's reported $46.1 billion in fiscal year 2010 active duty military payroll accounts for 20 percent of its net outlays.

Army Personnel Role in the Military Pay Process

The Under Secretary of Defense for Personnel and Readiness (USD (P&R)) advises the Secretary of Defense on a number of personnel areas such as recruitment, pay and benefits, and oversight of military readiness, and serves as DOD's Chief Human Capital Officer. The Office of the Assistant Secretary of the Army for Manpower and Reserve Affairs (ASA (M&RA)) is responsible for setting the strategic direction and providing overall supervision for manpower, personnel, and Reserve component affairs of the Department of the Army, and serves as the Army's lead for manpower policy and human resources, among other things. In order to fulfill these responsibilities, ASA (M&RA) relies on the Deputy Chief of Staff, G-1, for advice and assistance.[17] In addition to being the principal military advisor to ASA (M&RA), G-1's other responsibilities include developing policy that provides guidance for responsive and flexible human resources support of the Army and overseeing the officer accession and enlisted recruiting policy. The Human Resources Command supports the Deputy Chief of Staff, G-1, in the management of all military personnel by serving as the functional proponent for military personnel management and personnel systems. Army Human Resources Command, unit commanders, and training certification officials, among others, are responsible for providing DFAS-IN with accurate and timely information regarding changes in individual military member status necessary to maintain accurate and timely payroll accounts.

---

[15]Budgetary resources include the amount available to enter into new obligations and to liquidate them. Budgetary resources consist of new budget authority (including direct spending authority provided in existing statute and obligation limitations) and unobligated balances of budget authority provided in previous years.

[16]Offsetting collections are collections from intragovernmental transfers, business-like transactions with the public, and collections from the public that are governmental in nature but required by law to be classified as offsetting. These collections are all authorized by law to be credited to appropriation or fund expenditure accounts.

[17]The Deputy Chief of Staff, G-1 function also is referred to as Army Personnel.

Creation of a Military Pay Account

As illustrated in figure 1, military pay accounts are established as part of the enlistment process for new recruits and are based on personnel records. The recruiting office establishes the basics of the recruit's personnel file in the Army Recruiting Information Support System (ARISS). This file contains the recruit's full name, contact information, country of origin, social security number (SSN), and recruiting status. After applying, the recruit reports to a Military Entrance Processing Station (MEPS),[18] which works with the recruiting office to qualify applicants for military service and serves as the quality control unit between the recruiter and the military service. The applicant concludes the MEPS visit by signing either an enlistment contract or a delayed entry contract. The contract notes the terms of enlistment, such as pay grade, which relate to basic pay information. This completes the entrance documents that the MEPS collects. MEPS personnel then administer the Oath of Enlistment. All of the documents created are electronically transmitted to the respective service recruiting system, that is, ARISS for the Army, and a paper copy, referred to as a "Packet," is created that accompanies the recruit to the training installation where the Packet is delivered to the personnel office at the Reception Battalion.[19]

Recruits generally report to their assigned installation Reception Battalion for training within 2 weeks to 14 months after signing their enlistment contract. The service liaison counselor keeps the documentation Packet until the enlistee reports to the Reception Battalion, at which time the Packet is sent to the respective training installation. The Reception Battalion uses information contained in the Packet to create a personnel file in the Reception Battalion Automated Support System (RECBASS). The enlistee provides additional information on dependents, such as a marriage certificate, birth certificates for dependent children, and W-4 dependent information. Reception Battalion personnel staff assist the enlistee in filling out any additional forms if they were not included in the Packet, such as direct deposit, pay allotments for base housing, savings account deposits, child support, and emergency contact information.

---

[18]MEPS are under the U.S. Military Entrance Processing Command (USMEPCOM), which is the military entrance processing command for all Department of Defense military services and the U.S. Coast Guard. There are 65 MEPS within the United States and Puerto Rico.

[19]Some MEPS have moved to electronic records in lieu of hard copy Packets. Other MEPS may use Adobe Portable Document Format (PDF) file records that are e-mailed to the training installation.

GAO-12-406 Army Military Pay Audit Readiness

Personnel staff enter this information into the personnel system and send the information to the installation's Defense Military Pay Office where the enlistee's payroll account, referred to as a master military pay account, is created in DJMS-AC.[20]

Figure 1: Army Process for Creating a Military Pay Record for an Enlisted Service Member

1. Recruiting office visit

Prospective service member visits Army recruiting office.

2. Basic information

Recruiting office enters basic personnel information in ARISS.

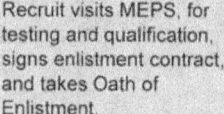

3. Military Entrance Processing Station (MEPS)

Recruit visits MEPS, for testing and qualification, signs enlistment contract, and takes Oath of Enlistment.

4. Enlistment packet

MEPS bundles qualifications information, enlistment contract, to create an enlistment Packet.

5. Enlistee and packet arrive

Enlistee and enlistment Packet arrive at training installation Reception Battalion, personnel office.

6. Personnel file created

Reception Battalion creates personnel file in RECBASS. Enlistee provides additional information, e.g., dependents.

7. Files sent to Defense Military Pay Office (DMPO)

Reception Battalion sends electronic or hard copy files to the DMPO for creation of a military pay account in DJMS.

8. Master Military Pay Account created

DMPO staff create service member's MMPA in DJMS-AC.

9. Pay record updated

Pay record is updated for changes in entitlement amounts based on special duties.

Source: GAO analysis of Army and DFAS processes.

Military pay starts once the payroll account is established in DJMS-AC. Army active duty military personnel receive pay and allowances based on their grade and time in service; location; and whether they are married, have dependents, or are performing special duties. The Army's active duty service members may elect to be paid once a month at the end of the month or twice a month at mid-month and at the end of month. The service member's pay information is consolidated into one monthly Leave and Earnings Statement. In addition to basic pay, military members may also be eligible for cash recruitment or retention incentives (i.e., bonuses). Any necessary pay change after the pay account is set up is initiated by

---

[20]Within the United States, DFAS-IN oversees 38 Defense Military Pay Offices and 14 satellite offices. Outside the United States, the Army Finance Command oversees 20 Finance Offices, which manage and update military pay accounts.

the appropriate officials throughout the Army. These changes generally relate to promotions, special duty pay, incentive pay, Permanent Change of Station assignments, Temporary Change of Station assignments, and changes in dependents.

The Defense Manpower Data Center (DMDC) is the central DOD source to identify, authenticate, authorize, and provide information on DOD-affiliated personnel. As such, it is the one, central access point for information and assistance on DOD entitlements, benefits, and medical readiness for uniformed service members, veterans, and their families. Major DMDC databases include information on pay; accessions and examinations (USMEPCOM); authorizations and requirements; military units and addresses, special purposes, for example, contingency operations; Joint Command duty assignments; retirement point repository; and mobilization/activations. DMDC has five major operating locations, including the DOD Center, in Monterey Bay, California; the Washington, D.C. area; and overseas locations in South Korea, Europe, and Southwest Asia. In addition, DMDC has 2,145 issuing stations (badge offices, etc.) at 1,400 worldwide locations. Computer support for the DOD Center in Monterey Bay is provided by the DOD Center in Monterey Bay and the Naval Postgraduate School in Monterey, California. Other computer support offices are located in Arlington, Virginia, and Auburn Hills, Michigan.

| Processing of Military Payroll | Payments of basic pay and allowances to service members are made via electronic funds transfer (EFT) through DJMS-AC.[21] At the local level, DMPOs are required to review any substantial changes (defined as +/- 150 percent) in payroll data daily. The intent of this review is to identify data input errors. In addition, a day before payroll is processed, DFAS-IN conducts a pre-payroll review. This is a manual process, where the DFAS-IN Military Pay Operations (Mil Pay Ops) staff obtain a sample[22] of Leave and Earnings Statements from DJMS-AC and trace the information in the statements to the relevant table outside of DJMS-AC. The purpose |

---

[21]Although most payments are EFTs to the service member, some payments may be made manually. For example, casual pay (an advance payment) may be made using a U.S. Treasury Check, cash, or stored value card (i.e., debit card).

[22]The number of Leave and Earnings Statements reviewed is dependent on the number of service members within DJMS-AC at that time. A program is run to select every 900th statement.

of this review is to identify potential system problems with the pay information used to calculate the pay amount. After completing this review, DFAS-IN then sends the DJMS-AC totals to the certifying official for certification. The certification process checks the DJMS-AC totals against the disbursing file totals. The certifying official sends an authorization and voucher to the Disbursing Office requesting release of payment. The DFAS-IN Disbursing Office uses the Army's disbursing system[23] to send electronic payments to the Federal Reserve Banks, which in turn distribute payments to each service member's bank account.

DFAS-IN's Accounting Division performs a number of steps to transfer payroll transactions from DJMS-AC to the Army's general ledger accounting system.[24] The Accounting Division receives DJMS reports from Mil Pay Ops that contain the computed total pay costs and disbursements for the payroll transactions, which are recorded as summary records by budget activity (e.g., officer, enlisted, and cadet pay). An individual soldier's payroll information is not recorded in the accounting system. Military pay accounting data is uploaded from the Army's general ledger accounting system into the Defense Departmental Reporting System-Budgetary (DDRS-B) for budgetary reporting and then to DDRS-Audited Financial Statement (DDRS-AFS) for financial statement reporting. Figure 2 provides a high-level illustration of the Army's complex environment for establishing military personnel and payroll records and processing military pay.

---

[23]The Army's disbursing system, Standard Financial System (STANFINS) Redesign Subsystem-1 (SRD-1), is an online, interactive accounting and finance system that incorporates Military Pay, Accounts Payable, Civilian Pay, Accounting and Disbursing into the online finance and accounting system.

[24]The Standard Financial System (STANFINS) is the Army standard general ledger system currently used for recording military payroll.

Figure 2: Overview of Major Systems Involved in Processing Active Army Military Payroll

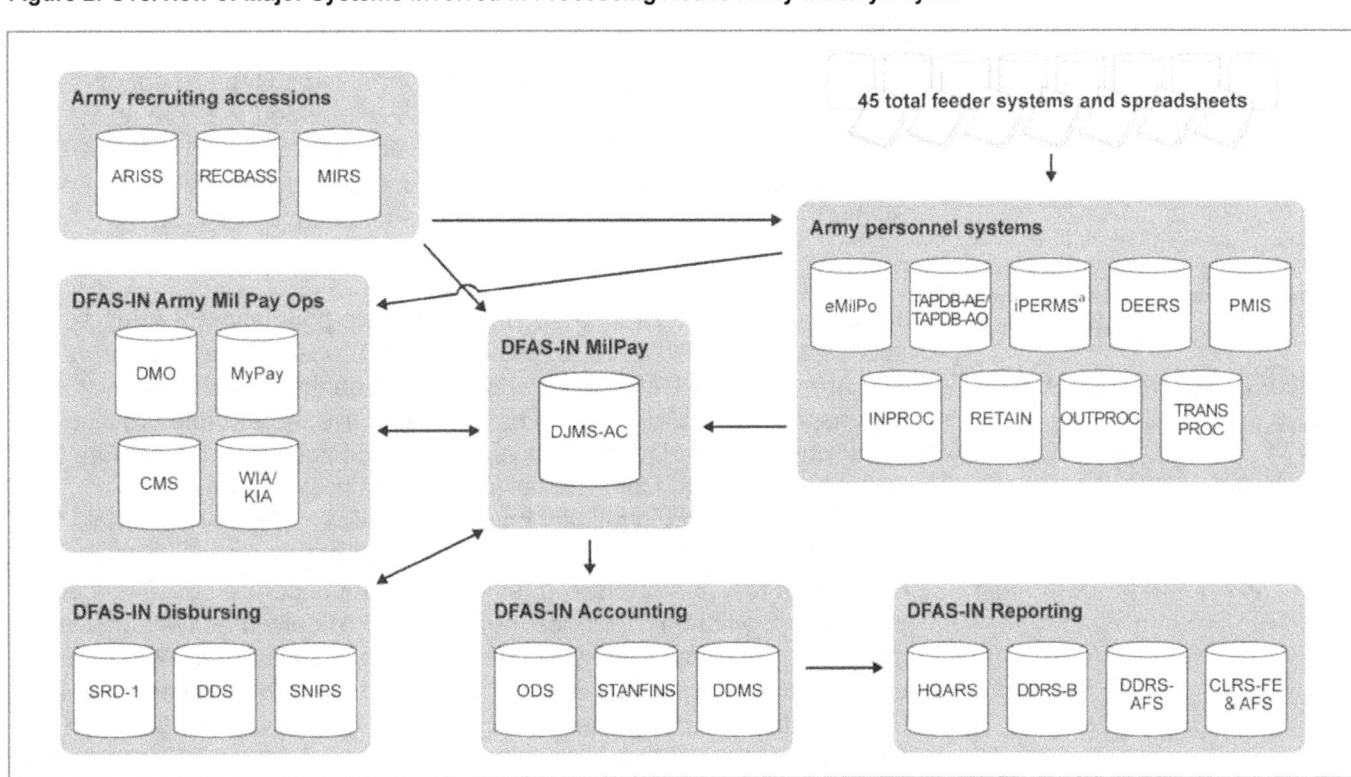

Accession
ARISS – Army Recruiting Information Support System
RECBASS – Reception Battalion Automated Support System
MIRS – U.S. Military Entrance Processing Command (USMEPCOM) Integrated Resource System

Personnel
eMILPO – electronic Military Personnel Office
TAPDB-AE/TAPDB-AO – Total Army Personnel Database-Active Enlisted/Active Officer
iPERMS – interactive Personnel Electronic Records Management System
DEERS – Defense Eligibility Enrollment Reporting System
PMIS – Personnel Management Information System
INPROC – In-Processing System
RETAIN – Reenlistment, Reclassification and Assignment System
OUTPROC – Out-Processing System
TRANSPROC – Military Personnel Transition Point Processing

DFAS-IN
DMO – Defense MilPay Office System
MyPay – My Pay (Individual soldier portal)
CMS – Case Management System
WIA/KIA – Wounded in Action/Killed in Action
DJMS-AC – Defense Joint Military Pay System – Active Component
ODS – Operational Data Store
STANFINS – Standard Finance System
DDMS – Defense Debt Management System
HQARS – Headquarters Accounting and Reporting System
DDRS-B – Defense Departmental Reporting System – Budgetary
DDRS-AFS – Defense Departmental Reporting System – Audited Financial Statements
CLRS-FE – CFO Load & Reconciliation System – Front End
CLRS-AFS – CFO Load & Reconciliation System – Audited Financial Statements
SRD-1 – Standard Finance System – Redesign 1
DDS – Deployable Disbursing System
SNIPS – Standard Negotiable Instruments Processing System

Source: GAO analysis of Army and DFAS-IN systems and process information.

[a]iPERMS does not feed DJMS-AC.

Army Regulation No. 600-8-104, Military Personnel Information Management/Records, establishes requirements for the Army's Official Military Personnel File.[25] The Army deployed iPERMS in 2007, and certain MilPer (Military Personnel) Messages and a Department of the Army memorandum indicate that iPERMS is intended to serve as the system of record for the Official Military Personnel File.[26] In addition, the Army is in the process of developing the Integrated Personnel and Pay System-Army (IPPS-A), which is targeted for completion in 2017.

Process and System Weaknesses Hindered Army's Ability to Identify a Valid Population of Military Payroll Transactions

The Army could not readily identify a complete population of Army payroll accounts for fiscal year 2010, given existing procedures and systems. The Army and the Defense Finance and Accounting Service in Indianapolis (DFAS-IN) did not have an effective, repeatable process for identifying the population of active duty payroll accounts. In addition, the Defense Manpower Data Center (DMDC) did not have an effective process for comparing military pay account files to military personnel files to identify a valid population of military payroll transactions.[27] For example, it took 3 months and repeated attempts before DFAS-IN could provide a population of service members who received active duty Army military pay in fiscal year 2010. Similarly, it took DMDC over 2 months to compare the total number of fiscal year 2010 active duty payroll accounts to its database of personnel files. *Standards for Internal Control in the Federal Government* requires all transactions and other significant events to be clearly documented and the documentation readily available for examination.[28] In addition, these ineffective processes are not in accord with DOD's own guidance or financial audit guidance. DOD's *Financial*

---

[25]Department of the Army, Army Regulation No. 600-8-104, *Military Personnel Information Management/Records* (Washington, D.C.: June 22, 2004).

[26]MilPer Message Number 10-322, "Submitting OMPF Documents into the Interactive Personnel Electronic Records System (iPERMS)," § 3, Dec. 9, 2010; MilPer Message Number 08-072, "Changes to Information Management Maintenance for the Official Military Personnel File (OMPF) and DA Form 201, Military Personnel Records Jacket (MPRJ)," §§ 2–5, March 18, 2008; and Department of the Army (DA) Memo 600-8-104, "Military Personnel Information Management/Records: Official Military Personnel File Access," §§ 1–6, June 26, 2006.

[27]DFAS-IN processes military payroll for the Army, and DMDC supports audits by performing analyses of Army military personnel files and data.

[28]GAO, *Standards for Internal Control in the Federal Government*, GAO/AIMD-00-21.3.1 (Washington, D.C.: November 1999).

Improvement and Audit Readiness (FIAR) Guidance sets out key tasks essential to achieving audit readiness, including defining and identifying the population of transactions for audit purposes.[29] The *GAO/PCIE Financial Audit Manual* (FAM) provides guidance concerning typical control activities, such as independent checks on the validity, accuracy, and completeness of computer-processed data.[30] One example of a control in this area includes comparing data from different sources for accuracy and completeness. Without effective processes for identifying a complete population of Army military pay records and comparing military pay accounts to personnel records, the Army will have difficulty meeting DOD's 2014 audit readiness goal and its 2017 goal for a complete set of auditable financial statements.

DFAS-IN Did Not Have an Effective Process for Identifying the Population of Army Military Payroll Records

DFAS-IN made three attempts from November 2010 through early January 2011 to provide us a Defense Joint Military Pay System-Active Component (DJMS-AC) file extract of Army service members who received active duty pay in fiscal year 2010. The first attempt included 11,940 duplicate pay accounts, and the total number of pay accounts included in the second attempt increased by 28,035 records over the first attempt, necessitating a third attempt to establish the population of fiscal year 2010 active duty pay records. We requested that DMDC compare the results of DFAS-IN's third attempt to identify the population of Army fiscal year 2010 payroll accounts against DMDC's compilation of monthly active duty payroll data that it received from DFAS-IN. Of the 677,024 Army active duty pay accounts, per DJMS-AC, we were able to reconcile all but 1,025 pay accounts (less than 1 percent of the total active duty pay accounts, which is not considered material) to pay account data that DFAS-IN had previously provided to DMDC. *Standards for Internal Control in the Federal Government* requires all transactions and other significant events to be clearly documented and the documentation

---

[29]DOD, Office of the Under Secretary of Defense (Comptroller/CFO), *Financial Improvement and Audit Readiness (FIAR) Guidance,* December 2011.

[30]GAO/PCIE, *Financial Audit Manual, Volume 1,* GAO-08-585G (Washington, D.C.: July 2008). The President's Council on Integrity and Efficiency (PCIE) was replaced by the Council of the Inspectors General on Integrity and Efficiency (CIGIE). CIGIE was statutorily established as an independent entity within the executive branch by the Inspector General Reform Act of 2008, Pub. L. No. 110-409, § 7, 122 Stat. 4302, 4305-4313 (Oct. 14, 2008) (codified at 5 U.S.C. App., § 11).

readily available for examination.[31] As discussed later in this report, we were unable to verify the validity of the records. Further, we did not attempt to reconcile military payroll amounts to the related disbursements because an Office of the Secretary of Defense (Comptroller) and Chief Financial Officer (OUSD(C)) contractor was in the process of performing a pilot reconciliation of payroll to disbursement data.

DOD's *Financial Improvement and Audit Readiness (FIAR) Guidance* states that being able to provide transaction-level detail for an account balance is a key task essential to achieving audit readiness. At the time we initiated our audit, Army officials told us that they had not yet focused on this area in their audit readiness efforts because the target date for Army military pay was not until the first quarter of fiscal year 2015.[32] The inability to readily provide a population of military pay accounts impeded our efforts to accomplish our audit objectives and, if not effectively addressed, will impede the Army's ability to meet DOD's new Statement of Budgetary Resources audit readiness goal of September 30, 2014.

System Weaknesses Hindered the Matching of Army Pay Accounts to Personnel Files

DMDC did not have an effective process for comparing military pay account files with military personnel files. The Army's pay and personnel systems are not integrated, which can lead to differences between the systems and potential errors. Therefore, an audit of military pay would include comparisons of military payroll accounts to personnel records to identify discrepancies. While DMDC was ultimately able to confirm that all 677,024 service members who received fiscal year 2010 active duty Army military pay from the DJMS-AC had an active duty personnel file in one of the multiple personnel systems, the reconciliation process was labor intensive and took over 2 months to complete. For example, DMDC's initial comparison of active duty Army military pay accounts to personnel records identified 67,243 pay accounts that did not have a corresponding active army personnel record on September 30, 2010.[33] Labor-intensive research was necessary to reconcile the differences between DJMS-AC pay records and Army personnel files compiled by DMDC. According to

---

[31]GAO/AIMD-00-21.3.1.

[32]Subsequent to this discussion, the Secretary of Defense issued a memo accelerating the Statement of Budgetary Resources audit readiness goal from 2017 to 2014.

[33]The personnel file used for comparison included service members who were still on active duty in the Army on September 30, 2010, and did not cover the entire fiscal year.

DMDC, these differences related primarily to personnel who had either left or were scheduled to leave the service, were reserve component soldiers released from active duty, or were soldiers who had died during fiscal year 2010. For these reasons, the service members were not included in the personnel file on September 30, 2010, that DMDC used for our initial comparison. We confirmed six duplicate SSNs in personnel records with the Social Security Administration and referred these records to DMDC and the Army for further research and appropriate action.[34]

DMDC attempted to complete our requested comparison of active duty Army pay accounts to military personnel records in January 2011, but was unable to complete the reconciliation until early March 2011. DMDC officials told us that the reasons for the delays included mainframe computer issues,[35] staff illness and turnover, and management data quality reviews of the file comparison results, including additional file comparisons to resolve differences. Without an effective process for confirming that the Army's active duty payroll population reconciles to military personnel records, the Army's efforts to meet DOD's Statement of Budgetary Resources auditability goal of September 30, 2014, will be impeded.

---

[34]The six duplicate personnel records related to SSNs that were assigned to two different service member names.

[35]DMDC and other DOD agencies use the Navy Postgraduate School mainframe computer to support their activities and share data processing priorities.

The Army Was Unable to Provide Documentation to Support the Validity and Accuracy of a Sample of Payroll Transactions

The Army does not have an efficient or effective process or system for providing documentation that supports payments for Army military payroll. For example, DFAS-IN had difficulty retrieving and providing usable Leave and Earnings Statements files for our sample items, and the Army and DFAS were unable to provide personnel and finance documents to support our statistical tests of all 250 service members' pay accounts for fiscal year 2010. *Standards for Internal Control in the Federal Government*[36] and DOD's FIAR Guidance[37] require audited entities to document transactions and events and assure that supporting documentation can be identified, located, and provided for examination. In addition, DOD Regulation 7000.14-R, *Financial Management Regulation* (FMR), requires the military components to maintain documentation supporting all data generated and input into finance and accounting systems or submitted to DFAS.[38] Further, DOD's *Financial Improvement and Audit Readiness (FIAR) Guidance* states that identifying and evaluating supporting documentation for individual transactions and balances, as well as identifying the location and sources of supporting documentation and confirming that appropriate supporting documentation exists, is a key audit readiness step. However, because the Army was unable to provide documents to support reported payroll amounts, we were unable to determine whether the Army's payroll accounts were valid, and we were unable to verify the accuracy of payments and reported active duty military payroll. Further, because military payroll is significant to the financial statements, the Army will not be able to pass an audit of its Statement of Budgetary Resources without resolving these control weaknesses. The following discussion summarizes the problems with the Army's processes related to military pay audit readiness.

---

[36]GAO, *Standards for Internal Control in the Federal Government*, GAO/AIMD-00-21.3.1 (Washington, D.C.: November 1999).

[37]DOD, Office of the Secretary of Under Secretary of Defense (Comptroller/CFO) *Financial Improvement and Audit Readiness (FIAR) Guidance,* December 2011.

[38]DOD, FMR, Volume 6A, Chapter 2, "Financial Reports Roles and Responsibilities," ¶ 020201.B. (rev. August 2011).

DFAS-IN Could Not Readily Provide Usable Leave and Earnings Statement Files for Sample Items

DFAS-IN staff experienced difficulty and delays in providing usable Leave and Earnings Statement files to support our testing of Army military payroll. We selected a sample of 250 service members and requested the relevant Leave and Earnings Statement files for fiscal year 2010. After multiple discussions and requests, we ultimately obtained usable Leave and Earnings Statement files for our sample items—5 weeks after our initial request. DFAS-IN took over 2 weeks to obtain the initial set of Leave and Earnings Statement files because it retrieves the files from two areas of the Defense Joint Military Pay System-Active Component (DJMS-AC). The active DJMS-AC database holds the current month plus the previous 12 months' data; older data are archived. When we requested Leave and Earnings Statement files for fiscal year 2010 in April 2011, a portion of these files had been archived and had to be retrieved from the archived database. In addition, the first set of Leave and Earnings Statement files that DFAS-IN provided included statements outside the requested fiscal year 2010 timeframe of our audit, thus we had to request a new set of files. It took over 1 week, including our data quality review, to obtain the second set of Leave and Earnings Statement files consisting of 445 separate files containing monthly statements for the 250 service member pay accounts in our sample. We determined that the Leave and Earnings Statements for an individual service member generally were in two or more of the files provided. Consequently, we had to combine these files into a format with each service member's Leave and Earnings Statement files grouped together to include all of the pay and allowance information for the service members in our sample. This combining and formatting required 2 additional weeks.

The Army Was Unable to Locate Supporting Documentation for Military Pay Account Sample Items

Although the Army deployed the Interactive Personnel Management System (iPERMS) as the Army's Official Military Personnel File in 2007 and the requirements for assuring that adequate supporting documentation is available for audit and examination are clearly defined, the Army did not have procedures in place to assure that its military pay transactions were adequately supported and that the supporting documentation could be readily retrieved and provided for financial audit purposes. *Standards for Internal Control in the Federal Government* requires internal control and all transactions and other significant events to be clearly documented and the documentation readily available for examination.[39] DOD Regulation 7000.14-R, *Financial Management*

---

[39]GAO/AIMD-00-21.3.1.

Regulation (FMR), requires the military components to maintain documentation supporting all data generated and input into finance and accounting systems or submitted to DFAS.[40] This regulation also requires the components to ensure that audit trails are maintained in sufficient detail to permit tracing of transactions from their sources to their transmission to DFAS. Audit trails are necessary to demonstrate the accuracy, completeness, and timeliness of transactions as well as to provide documentary support for all data generated by the component and submitted to DFAS for recording in the accounting systems and use in financial reports.[41] Further, DOD's FIAR Guidance states that identifying and evaluating supporting documentation for individual transactions and balances, as well as the location and sources of supporting documentation and confirming that appropriate supporting documentation exists, is a key audit readiness step.[42] Without the capability to readily locate and provide supporting documentation for military payroll transactions within a short timeframe, the Army's ability to pass a financial statement audit will be impeded.

After selecting our sample of 250 Army military payroll accounts in March 2011, we worked with Army Human Resources Command, Army Finance Command, and DFAS-IN officials to obtain source documents that supported basic pay, allowances, and entitlements. After being directed to make our document requests to various offices, none of which provided supporting documentation but instead referred us to other offices, we suggested that the Army focus on the first 20 pay account sample items to assess the feasibility of obtaining supporting documentation.[43] When the Army continued to have difficulty locating supporting documentation, we suggested that the Army focus on the first 5 sample items. As of the end of September 2011, 6 months after receiving our initial request, the Army and DFAS-IN were able to provide complete documentation for 2 of

---

[40]DOD, FMR, Volume 6A, Chapter 2, "Financial Reports Roles and Responsibilities," 020201.B. (rev. August 2011).

[41]DOD, FMR, Volume 6A, Chapter 2, "Financial Reports Roles and Responsibilities," 020203.A. (rev. August 2011); GAO/AIMD-00-21.3.1.

[42]DOD, *Fiscal Year 2010 Financial Improvement and Audit Readiness (FIAR) Guidance,* Office of the Under Secretary of Defense (Comptroller/CFO) (Arlington, VA: May 15, 2010).

[43]A sample item constitutes a soldier's pay account for fiscal year 2010, including reported Leave and Earnings Statements for all 12 months of the fiscal year.

our 250 sample items, partial support for 3 sample items, and no support for the remaining 245 sample items.[44] Our review of the partial documentation provided for 3 sample items showed that the Army was unable to provide supporting documentation for common elements of its military pay, including basic allowance for housing, cost of living allowance, hardship duty pay-location, and hostile fire/imminent danger pay. Specifically,

- The Army was unable to provide supporting documentation for basic allowance for housing for one service member. In general, a service member on active duty is authorized a housing allowance based on the member's grade, dependency status, and location. Basic allowance for housing is based on the median housing costs and is paid independently of the service member's actual housing costs. At the conclusion of our fieldwork, a DFAS-IN official told us they had requested this documentation from the National Archives and Records Administration (NARA); however, they had not yet received it.[45]

- For two sample items, the Army did not provide adequate documentation that the two service members were appropriately paid for clothing allowance. A clothing allowance is paid to enlisted service members annually in the anniversary month each year after they received their first clothing allowance. At the end of our field work, DFAS-IN had not provided an explanation as to why these service members received their clothing allowance in a month other than their anniversary date.

- The Army was unable to provide supporting documentation for one service member residing within the continental United States receiving a cost-of-living allowance. A cost-of-living allowance for soldiers stationed in the United States is a supplemental allowance designed to help offset higher prices in high-cost locations. At the end of our field work, a DFAS-IN official told us they had requested the documentation from NARA; however, they had not yet received it.

---

[44]We used the results of DMDC's comparison of the population of Army fiscal year 2010 active duty military pay accounts to military personnel records to select a statistical sample of pay accounts for testing the accuracy of basic pay and allowance transactions reported on the related monthly fiscal year 2010 Leave and Earnings Statements.

[45]NARA is the nation's record keeper of all documents and materials created in the course of business conducted by the United States federal government.

- Finally, for two service members, the Army was unable to provide supporting documentation for hardship duty pay and hostile fire/imminent danger pay. Service members are entitled to hardship duty pay for location assignments when there is a permanent change of station duty or temporary/deployed/attached duty of over 30 days in a specific location. Additionally, a service member is entitled to hostile fire/imminent danger pay when, as certified by the appropriate commander, the member is (1) subject to hostile fire or explosion of a hostile mine; (2) on duty in an area close to hostile fire incidents and the member is in danger of being exposed to the same dangers experienced by other service members; or (3) killed, injured, or wounded by hostile fire and the service member is on official duty in a designated imminent danger pay area. At the end of our field work, the Army was unable to provide adequate support for the dates that each of these service members reported for duty at the specified location which triggered the start of these two types of pay, and it was unable to provide documentation that one service member had been ordered to report to duty in the designated location.

As shown in figure 3, the Army provided complete documentation for soldier pay accounts associated with sample items #2 and #4, but it was unable to provide complete documentation for sample items #1, #3, and #5. Further, after 6 months, the Army was still unable to provide any documentation for the remaining 245 pay account sample items.

Figure 3: Test Results for 5 of 250 Soldier Pay Account Sample Items

Type of pay or allowance	Item #1	Item #2	Item #3	Item #4	Item #5
Basic pay	✓	✓	✓	✓	✓
Basic allowance for subsistence (BAS)	✓	✓	✓	✓	✓
Basic allowance for housing (BAH)	✗	✓	✓	✓	✓
Clothing allowance	✗	✓	✗	N/A	✓
Family separation allowance (FSA)	N/A	N/A	✓	N/A	N/A
Overseas housing allowance (OHA)	N/A	N/A	N/A	✓	N/A
Dual overseas housing allowance (DUAL OHA)	N/A	N/A	N/A	✓	N/A
CONUS cost of living allowance (COLA)	✗	N/A	N/A	N/A	N/A
Cost of living allowance (COLA)	N/A	✓	N/A	✓	N/A
Special Duty Pay	✓	N/A	N/A	N/A	N/A
Hardship duty pay - location (HDP LOC)	N/A	N/A	✗	N/A	✗
Hostile Fire/Imminent Danger Pay (HFP/IDP)	N/A	N/A	✗	N/A	✗

✓   Adequate supporting documentation was provided   ✗   Adequate supporting documentation was not provided

N/A   Not applicable because the service member did not have this type of pay or allowance

Source: GAO analysis of Army documentation.

One of the reasons the Army was unable to provide supporting documentation is that it does not have a centralized repository for pay-affecting documents. Army personnel and finance documentation supporting basic pay and allowances resides in numerous systems, and original hard copy documents are scattered across the country—at hundreds of Army units and NARA federal records centers. According to Army and DFAS-IN officials, there are at least 45 separate systems that the Army uses to perform personnel and pay functions with no single, overarching personnel system. Although these systems contain personnel data on military members and their dependents and feed these data to DJMS-AC, the systems do not contain source documents.

Army Regulation No. 600-8-104, *Military Personnel Information Management/Records*, establishes requirements for the Army's Official Military Personnel File.[46] Army policies indicate that iPERMS is intended

---

[46]Department of the Army, Army Regulation No. 600-8-104, *Military Personnel Information Management/Records* (Washington, D.C.: June 22, 2004).

to serve as the system of record for the Official Military Personnel File.[47] The Army deployed iPERMS in 2007 and designated iPERMS as the Army's Official Military Personnel File. However, when we attempted to find supporting documents in iPERMS, we found that this system had not been consistently populated with the required service member documents, resulting in incomplete personnel records. For example, when attempting to test our sample, we discovered that documents, such as orders to support a special duty assignment, permanent change of station orders, and release or discharge from active duty, that should have been in iPERMS were not. The Army has designated the Human Resources Command as the owner of iPERMS; however, local installation personnel offices across the country are responsible for entering most documents into individual service member iPERMS accounts, and the Army has not established a mechanism for periodic monitoring, review, and accountability of iPERMS to ensure that personnel files are complete. For example, we found that documents needed to support pay transactions are not in iPERMS because (1) Army Regulation 600-8-104 does not require the personnel form to be included and (2) the documents are finance documents and not personnel documents.[48]

Efforts to achieve auditablity are further compounded by payroll system limitations. DJMS–AC, used to process Army active duty military pay, is an aging, Common Business Oriented Language (COBOL)[49] mainframe-based system that has had minimum system maintenance because DOD planned to transition to the Forward Capability Pay System and then to

---

[47]MilPer Message Number 10-322, "Submitting OMPF Documents into the Interactive Personnel Electronic Records System (iPERMS)," § 3, Dec. 9, 2010; MilPer Message Number 08-072, "Changes to Information Management Maintenance for the Official Military Personnel File (OMPF) and DA Form 201, Military Personnel Records Jacket (MPRJ)," §§ 2–5, March 18, 2008; and Department of the Army (DA) Memo 600-8-104, "Military Personnel Information Management/Records: Official Military Personnel File Access," §§ 1–6, June 26, 2006.

[48]These documents include the Department of the Army (DA) Form 5960, Authorization to Start, Stop or Change Basic Allowance for Quarters and/or Variable Housing Allowance; the Department of Defense (DD) Form 1561, Statement to Substantiate Payment of Family Separation Allowance (FSA); and the DD Form 2367, Individual Overseas Housing Allowance.

[49]COBOL is one of the earliest high-level programming languages. It was developed in 1959, and the language continues to evolve.

the Defense Integrated Military Human Resources System (DIMHRS).[50] DJMS-AC lacks key payroll computation abilities to pay active duty Army service members. To address these functionality limitations, DFAS has developed approximately 70 workaround procedures that are currently being used to compensate for the lack of functionality in DJMS-AC. An audit of Army military pay would necessitate an evaluation of these procedures and related controls.

Another factor in the Army's inability to provide support for military payroll is that the Army has not adequately documented its personnel processes and controls related to military pay. During our audit, we spent considerable time attempting to identify the range of personnel and finance documents that would be needed to support basic military pay and allowances reported on service members' Leave and Earnings Statements and the appropriate office responsible for providing the documentation. According to Internal Control Standards, written documentation should exist covering the agency's internal control structure and all significant transactions and events.[51] The documentation for internal control includes identification of the agency's activity-level functions and related objectives and control activities and should appear in management directives, administrative policies, accounting manuals, and other such guidance.

Army Military Pay Audit Readiness Efforts Currently Under Way

DOD's November 2011 FIAR Status Report includes DOD's goal of achieving audit readiness for its Statement of Budgetary Resources by the end of fiscal year 2014. DOD and the Army have established interim goals for meeting the fiscal year 2014 Statement of Budgetary Resources audit readiness goal. For example, the Army plans to assert audit readiness for its General Fund Statement of Budgetary Resources, including military pay, by March 31, 2013, and have its assertion tested and fully validated by June 30, 2014. Army officials stated that military pay audit readiness poses a significant challenge and acknowledged that

---

[50]The Defense Integrated Military Human Resources System (DIMHRS) was terminated due to the differences in the business processes, operations, and information required by each Service.

[51]GAO, *Standards for Internal Control in the Federal Government*, GAO/AIMD-00-21.3.1 (Washington, D.C.: November 1999).

the success of the Army's efforts will be key to meeting DOD's 2014 Statement of Budgetary Resources audit readiness goal.

To meet this goal, the Army has several military pay audit readiness efforts planned or under way—most of which were begun after we initiated our audit. However, many of these efforts are in the early planning stages and will need to be carefully documented and managed to ensure effective and timely implementation.

- In November 2010, as part of the Office of the Under Secretary of Defense (Comptroller) (OUSD(C)) effort to provide management consulting assistance where needed on financial audit readiness, DOD provided contractor support to the Army for documenting and testing DJMS-AC application system controls.[52] In November 2011, OUSD(C) and contractor officials provided us a status briefing that indicated DOD's contractor expects to complete documentation and testing of DJMS-AC controls in March 2012.

- The November 2011 OUSD(C) status briefing also noted that the Army's Financial Improvement Plan (FIP) team began executing discovery, documentation, and controls testing of front-end military pay business processes, including accessions; field service activities; and Military Personnel, Army appropriation budget activities. This effort includes processes executed by the Army financial management and personnel communities, including the Army Budget Office, Office of the Deputy Chief of Staff for Personnel, Army and DFAS installation finance and military pay offices, and Army installation military personnel offices. The Army FIP effort encompasses the active Army, Army National Guard, and U.S. Army Reserve. The Army plans to complete these efforts by December 31, 2012, and implement any required corrective actions by December 31, 2013.

  Further, as part of the Army FIP discovery effort, Army officials told us they plan to develop a repository of military pay entitlement information by entitlement type, which includes governing laws and regulations; the necessary key supporting documentation, responsible parties, and location for retrieval; as well as the automated information

---

[52]Application system control is a category of control designed to help ensure completeness, accuracy, validity, confidentiality, and availability of transactions and data during application processing.

systems involved and their owners. The Army plans to complete these efforts by December 31, 2013. However, it is not yet clear who will be responsible for entering pay-supporting documents in the repository and what process will be used for ensuring completeness of the files. As previously discussed, Army Regulation No. 600-8-104, *Military Personnel Information Management/Records*, established requirements for the Official Military Personnel File, but the regulation did not include requirements for ensuring that personnel documents are centrally located, retained in the service members' Official Military Personnel File, or otherwise readily accessible. The regulation also did not require that these files be monitored to ensure their completeness.

- Army officials told us that in conjunction with DFAS, it has identified other systems for SSAE No. 16[53] and DFAS self-reviews. Further, the Army plans to identify by March 31, 2012, all systems that have a material impact on the military pay processes and require *Federal Information System Controls Audit Manual* (FISCAM) assessments.[54] The Army intends that all required reviews will be completed by December 31, 2013.

  Additionally, the Army is working with DFAS-IN to document processes and perform control testing of payroll accounting, referred to by the Army as back-end processes. The Army expects to implement all corrective actions on these controls by December 31, 2012.

- As a result of our work, Army and DFAS-IN officials told us they plan to develop a matrix of personnel documents that support military pay and allowances and identify officials responsible for providing this documentation. Army Deputy Chief of Staff, G-1, officials plan to work with IPPS-A team members to determine how IPPS-A will incorporate or link to this information. Effective development of such a matrix will be critical to ensuring that payroll transactions are supported and,

---

[53]Statement on Standards for Attestation Engagements (SSAE) No. 16,"Reporting on Controls for a Service Organization," effective July 15, 2011, supersedes Statements on Auditing Standards (SAS) No. 70, and provides professional guidance on performing the service provider's (e.g., DFAS) examination.

[54]GAO, *Federal Information System Controls Audit Manual (FISCAM)*, GAO-09-232G (Washington, D.C.: Feb. 2, 2009). See §1.1 for purpose and use of the FISCAM.

therefore, audit ready. The need for such a matrix became apparent nearly 1 year ago, but the Army has not yet completed such a matrix or identified personnel responsible for providing needed documents. Further, it has not established a central repository for these documents, or designated iPERMS as the official repository, and it has not established a mechanism for periodic monitoring, review, and accountability to ensure that the central repository will be effectively maintained.

- In addition, the Army is in the process of developing the Integrated Personnel and Pay System-Army (IPPS-A). However, the current targeted IPPS-A implementation date of 2017 will require the Army to rely on its current systems for purposes of meeting DOD's Statement of Budgetary Resources audit readiness date of September 30, 2014. IPPS–A is planned to be developed and implemented in two increments, with multiple releases. The Army plans to employ 14- to 18-month development cycles for each release, with the goal of fielding capabilities every 12 months. The Army intends for Increment I to consist of a trusted data source of soldier personnel and human resource data and to provide the foundation for Increment II, which is expected to provide integrated personnel and pay services, to be developed and implemented across multiple releases. In response to our findings in this report, Army IPPS-A officials told us that they have recently begun efforts to determine how IPPS-A will link to personnel records that will be needed to support Army military payroll amounts. The Army's strategy is for each release of IPPS-A to incrementally build upon the prior release's design and capability, to ultimately contribute toward the Army's goal of reaching financial auditability by fiscal year 2017. Because implementation of the IPPS-A is not targeted for completion until 2017, a slippage in the implementation date could impede the Army's efforts to support DOD's financial statement audit readiness goal of September 30, 2017. Without timely and effective efforts to establish an electronic repository of pay-supporting documents and ensure that the documentation is complete, IPPS-A will not be able to fully support the Army's audit readiness efforts.

Conclusions

Active Army military payroll, reported at $46.1 billion for fiscal year 2010, is material to all of the Army's financial statements, and as such, will be significant to the Army's audit readiness goals for the Statement of Budgetary Resources. The Army has several military pay audit readiness efforts that are planned or under way. Timely and effective implementation of these efforts could help reduce the risk related to

DOD's 2014 Statement of Budgetary Resources audit readiness goal. However, most of these actions are in the early planning stages. Moreover, these initiatives, while important, do not address (1) establishing effective processes and systems for identifying a valid population of military payroll records, (2) ensuring Leave and Earnings Statement files and supporting personnel documents are readily available for verifying the accuracy of payroll records, (3) ensuring key personnel and other pay-related documents that support military payroll transactions are centrally located, retained in service member Official Military Personnel Files, or otherwise readily accessible, and (4) requiring the Army's Human Resources Command to periodically review and confirm that service member Official Military Personnel File records in iPERMS or other master personnel record systems are consistent and complete to support annual financial audit requirements. These same issues, if not effectively resolved, could also jeopardize the 2017 goal for audit readiness on the complete set of DOD financial statements. In addition, the Army's military pay auditability weaknesses have departmentwide implications as the other military components, such as the Air Force and the Navy, share some of the same military pay process and systems risks as the Army. Going forward, focused and committed leadership and knowledgeable staff in key functional areas, including personnel, systems, military payroll, and accounting will be essential to effective implementation of military pay audit readiness efforts.

Recommendations for Executive Action

To help the Army develop the processes and controls necessary to achieve financial statement audit readiness for military pay, we are making the following four recommendations.

We recommend that the Secretary of the Army direct the Assistant Secretary of the Army for Financial Management and Comptroller to work with Army Personnel (G-1), DFAS-IN, and audit readiness officials to

- document and implement a process for identifying and validating the population of payroll transactions for fiscal year periods at a minimum.

- identify key finance (i.e., pay-affecting) documents that support military payroll transactions and develop and implement procedures for maintaining them, including responsibility for coordination with Army Personnel (G-1) and audit readiness officials.

In addition, we recommend that the Secretary of the Army direct the Assistant Secretary of the Army for Manpower and Reserve Affairs to revise AR No. 600-8-104, *Military Personnel Information Management/Records,* to require that

- key personnel and other pay-related documents that support military payroll transactions are centrally located, retained in the service members' Official Military Personnel File, or otherwise readily accessible. Consider first using the Interactive Personnel Management System (iPERMS) for this purpose.

- the Army's Human Resources Command periodically review and confirm that service member Official Military Personnel File records in iPERMS or other master personnel record systems are consistent and complete to support annual financial audit requirements.

Agency Comments and Our Evaluation

We received written comments from the Secretary of the Army on March 12, 2012, stating that the Army agreed with our four recommendations. The Army's letter also states that our work has been extremely helpful in identifying the need to have consistent agreed-upon rules for documenting files required to support audits of military pay and cited several efforts under way to improve the auditability of its military pay. The Army's comments are reprinted in appendix II.

The Army's letter states that it believes we found no significant issues in our review of the military pay accounts, but our report is very clear in highlighting the significance of the issues with the Army's military payroll. For instance, our report states that without effective processes for identifying a complete population of Army military pay records and comparing military pay accounts to personnel records, the Army will have difficulty meeting DOD's 2014 Statement of Budgetary Resources audit readiness goal and its 2017 goal for a complete set of auditable financial statements. In addition, because the Army was unable to provide documents to support reported payroll amounts, we were unable to determine whether the Army's payroll accounts were valid, and we were unable to verify the accuracy of the payments and reported active duty military payroll.

Further, in responding to our first recommendation that the Army document and implement a process for identifying and validating the population of payroll transactions for fiscal year periods, the Army stated that it validates personnel and payroll records monthly in real time, and will evaluate the value of retaining personnel files for prior years. If the monthly pay to personnel comparison is a control procedure that the Army performs regularly and intends for the auditors to rely on, the process and results must be documented and retained for the auditor to assess and test beyond the end of the fiscal year, as we recommended.

We are sending copies of this report to the Secretary of Defense; the Under Secretary of Defense (Comptroller/Chief Financial Officer); the Deputy Chief Financial Officer; the Director, Financial Improvement and Audit Readiness; the Secretary of the Army; the Assistant Secretary of the Army for Financial Management and Comptroller; the Assistant Secretary of the Army for Manpower and Reserve Affairs; the Director of Army Finance Command; the Directors of DFAS and the DFAS-Indianapolis Center; the Director of the Defense Manpower Data Center; the Director of the Office of Management and Budget; and appropriate congressional committees. In addition, the report is available at no charge on the GAO website at http://www.gao.gov.

If you or your staffs have any questions about this report, please contact me at (202) 512-9869 or khana@gao.gov. Contact points for our Office of Congressional Relations and Public Affairs may be found on the last page of this report. GAO staff who made major contributions to this report are listed in appendix III.

Asif A. Khan
Director, Financial Management and Assurance

List of Committees

The Honorable Thomas R. Carper
Chairman
The Honorable Scott P. Brown
Ranking Member
Subcommittee on Federal Financial
Management, Government Information,
Federal Services, and International Security
Committee on Homeland Security and Governmental Affairs
United States Senate

The Honorable Claire McCaskill
Chairman
Subcommittee on Contracting Oversight
Committee on Homeland Security and Governmental Affairs
United States Senate

The Honorable Tom Coburn
Ranking Member
Permanent Subcommittee on Investigations
Committee on Homeland Security and Governmental Affairs
United States Senate

The Honorable Todd Platts
Chairman
The Honorable Edolphus Towns
Ranking Member
Subcommittee on Government Organization,
Efficiency and Financial Management
Committee on Oversight and Government Reform
United States House of Representatives

Appendix I: Objectives, Scope, and Methodology

This audit was initiated under our mandate to audit the consolidated financial statements of the United States government.[1] Our objectives were to perform basic audit procedures necessary to conclude about the validity and accuracy of Army's active duty military payroll. Those basic audit procedures included (1) identifying a valid population of military payroll transactions, and (2) testing a sample of payroll transactions for validity and accuracy.

To identify the population of Army active duty payroll transactions, we obtained Army active duty military payroll records from the Defense Finance and Accounting Service, Indianapolis (DFAS-IN). DFAS-IN processes military payroll for the Army. At our request, DFAS-IN made three attempts from November 2010 through January 2011 to provide us a complete file of service members who were paid in fiscal year 2010. The first attempt included 11,940 pay accounts that were duplicate, and the total number of pay accounts included in the second attempt increased by 28,035 records over the first attempt, necessitating a third request for the population of fiscal year 2010 active duty pay records. To obtain assurance that the overall population of Army fiscal year 2010 payroll accounts matched the sum of monthly payroll accounts, we requested the Defense Manpower Data Center (DMDC) compare the results of our third request for the population of Army fiscal year 2010 payroll accounts against its compilation of monthly active duty payroll data that it received from DFAS-IN. We were able to reconcile all but 1,025 pay accounts (less than 1 percent of the total, which is not considered material). We did not reconcile military payroll amounts to the related disbursements because an Office of the Under Secretary of Defense (Comptroller) and Chief Financial Officer (OUSD(C)) contractor was in the process of performing a pilot reconciliation.

In addition, because the Army does not have an integrated military personnel and payroll system, we worked with the DMDC to match payroll accounts to personnel records to determine whether the population of Army military payroll accounts was in agreement with the population in the DMDC database.[2] We relied on work performed by DMDC because

---

[1]31 U.S.C. §§ 331(e), 717(b)(1).

[2]DFAS-IN's third population attempt identified 677,024 active duty Army Service members (excluding those who were assigned to classified duties). We excluded soldiers assigned to classified duties from our audit scope.

we reviewed its quality control procedures and found them to be
adequate, for our purposes. We compared the total number of records in
DFAS-IN's population and DMDC's database for the service members
who received active duty Army military pay in fiscal year 2010. We did not
separately validate Army personnel file data. DMDC's file comparison of
Army active duty pay accounts to military personnel records identified
67,243 pay accounts that were not matched to a file of military personnel
records on September 30, 2010. We asked DMDC to perform more
detailed comparisons of these differences. These differences related
primarily to personnel who were not active Army service members
because they had either left or were scheduled to leave the service, were
reserve component soldiers released from active duty, or were soldiers
that had died during fiscal year 2010. Finally, we confirmed six duplicate
SSNs in personnel records with different names with the Social Security
Administration and referred these records to DMDC and the Army for
further research and appropriate action.

To address our second objective, we documented key controls, laws, and
pay regulations and used the population of matched personnel and
payroll records to select a statistical sample of 250 soldiers for testing the
accuracy and validity of Army military payroll.[3] We obtained 12 months of
fiscal year 2010 Leave and Earnings Statement files for each soldier in
our sample, the most recent data available at the time, to compare with
supporting Army personnel documents indicating such information as
military orders, special duty and expertise entitlements, marital status,
and dependent information. We gained an understanding of Army
processes with a focus on key steps involved in establishing military
personnel records related to specific pay and allowance amounts. We
also performed process walkthroughs at DFAS-IN and assessed key
controls over the accuracy of payroll payments made to service members.
To document the process for capturing pay-related information and
setting up military personnel records, we interviewed Army personnel,
Human Resources Command, and Finance Command officials and
visited a Military Enlistment Program Station in Indianapolis and a military
reception battalion at Fort Jackson, South Carolina. We also interviewed
finance officials at Defense Military Pay Offices at Fort Jackson, South
Carolina, and Fort Carson, Colorado, to gain an understanding of how

---

[3]Our sampling plan was based on a 95-percent confidence interval and had an acceptable
error rate of 5 percent.

pay adjustments are initiated, input, and reviewed. We requested and
obtained fiscal year 2010 monthly Leave and Earnings Statement files for
the service members in our sample from DFAS-IN and requested Army
personnel documents to support basic pay and allowance amounts
reported on the Leave and Earnings Statements, including such
information as military orders, and the certifications of special duty
expertise, marital status, and dependent information. We did not plan to,
nor did we test deductions and allotments for items such as Service
Member's Group Life Insurance, Thrift Savings Plan, and TRICARE. In
addition to basic pay, we planned to test base housing allowance;
hazardous duty pay; hostile fire/imminent danger pay; cost of living
allowance; military overseas housing allowance; family separation
housing; temporary lodging allowance; clothing allowance; and special
duty pay, such as foreign language proficiency pay and parachute (jump)
pay. We reviewed documentation provided by the Army for 5 sample
items and documentation contained in the Army's Interactive Personnel
Management System (iPERMS), which serves as the Army's Official
Military Personnel File. We were unable to complete our tests of active
duty military payroll accuracy because of a scope limitation related to the
Army's inability to provide support for its active component military payroll
transactions.

In support of our objectives, we reviewed Army military personnel and
payroll policies and procedures and identified sources of pay-related
documentation. Throughout our work, we interviewed key Army officials in
Manpower and Reserve Affairs, Human Resources Command, and
Finance Command. We also interviewed DFAS-IN officials responsible for
payroll functions and Office of the Under Secretary of Defense
(Comptroller/Chief Financial Officer) audit readiness contractor officials.
Additionally, we interviewed agency officials regarding the status of
Army's efforts to develop an Integrated Personnel and Payroll System-
Army (IPPS-A). We also performed walkthroughs of DFAS-IN Military Pay
Operations, accounting, disbursing, financial reporting, and related
processes.

We conducted this performance audit from June 2010 through March
2012 in accordance with generally accepted government auditing
standards. Those standards require that we plan and perform the audit to
obtain sufficient, appropriate evidence to provide a reasonable basis for
our findings and conclusions based on our audit objectives. We believe
that the evidence obtained provides a reasonable basis for our findings
and conclusions based on our audit objectives. Other matters identified in

our work that merit management's attention and correction will be
reported in a separate letter to Army management.

Appendix II: Comments from the Department of the Army

SECRETARY OF THE ARMY
WASHINGTON

1 2 MAR 2012

MEMORANDUM FOR Director, Financial Management and Assurance, U.S. Government Accountability Office, 441 G Street, NW, Washington, DC 20548

SUBJECT: Government Accountability Office Draft Report (GAO-12-406), 'DOD Financial Management: The Army Faces Significant Challenges in Achieving Audit Readiness for Its Military Pay'

1. I am pleased to provide the following Department of Defense (DOD) response to the GAO Draft Report, GAO-12-406, 'DOD Financial Management: The Army Faces Significant Challenges in Achieving Audit Readiness for Its Military Pay,' dated 8 February 2012 (GAO Code 198649).

2. We appreciate your confirmation that no significant issues were identified in your review of the military pay accounts for the Army and understand the challenges in rapidly obtaining documents and files from prior periods to support audit populations for sampling. It should be noted that the Army does have an ongoing process for comparing payroll and personnel records; however, this is done directly with the Army personnel systems rather than the Defense Data Management Center, as used by the auditors. This review has been extremely helpful in identifying the need to have consistent, agreed-upon rules of the documentation and files required to support audits of military pay data in the payroll system as part of overall financial audits. As noted in the report, our audit readiness team is developing comprehensive documentation of the processes and controls within the military pay area. Documentation requirements are an essential part of this effort, as automated and manual controls often provide better assurance of transaction validity than paper documents.

3. Enclosed are specific responses to the report recommendations. Please extend our appreciation to your auditors for the work performed. My point of contact for this matter is Mr. G. Eric Reid at eric.reid@dfas.mil or telephone (317) 510-2223.

John M. McHugh

Encl

GOVERNMENT ACCOUNTABILITY OFFICE (GAO) DRAFT REPORT DATED
FEBRUARY 9, 2012
GAO-12-406 (GAO CODE 198649)

"DOD FINANCIAL MANAGEMENT: THE ARMY FACES SIGNIFICANT
CHALLENGES
IN ACHIEVING AUDIT READINESS FOR ITS MILITARY PAY"

DEPARTMENT OF ARMY COMMENTS
TO THE GAO RECOMMENDATIONS

RECOMMENDATION 1: The Secretary of the Army direct the Assistant Secretary of the
Army for Financial Management and Comptroller work with Army Personnel (G-1),
Defense Finance and Accounting Service (DFAS), and audit readiness officials to
document and implement a process for identifying and validating the population of
payroll transactions for fiscal year periods at a minimum.

DoD RESPONSE: Concur. The Army will work with DFAS to retain readily accessible
historical payroll files by fiscal year for support of establishing automated populations for
audit sampling. Because validation between personnel and payroll records is done
monthly in real time, the value of retaining personnel files for prior years to duplicate this
process will be evaluated as part of the overall documentation of the processes and
controls for military pay. ECD: June 30, 2013

RECOMMENDATION 2: The Secretary of the Army direct the Assistant Secretary of the
Army for Financial Management and Comptroller work with Army Personnel (G-1),
Defense Finance and Accounting Service (DFAS), and audit readiness officials to
identify key finance (i.e., pay-related) documents that support military payroll
transactions and develop and implement procedures for maintaining them, including
responsibility for coordination with Army Personnel (G-1) and audit readiness officials.

DoD RESPONSE: Concur. The Army and DFAS are currently documenting the
processes and controls associated with military pay. As part of this effort, a matrix of
each entitlement, supporting substantiating document, and point of retention of those
documents is being developed. ECD: June 30, 2013

RECOMMENDATION 3: The Secretary of the Army direct the Assistant Secretary of
the Army for Manpower and Reserve Affairs to revise Army Regulation 600-8-104,
Military Personnel Information Management/Records, to require that key personnel and
other pay-related documents that support military payroll transactions are centrally

- 1 -

located, retained in the service members' Official Military Personnel File, or otherwise readily accessible. Consider first using the Interactive Personnel Management System (iPERMS) for this purpose.

DoD RESPONSE: Concur. ECD: June 30, 2013

RECOMMENDATION 4: The Secretary of the Army direct the Assistant Secretary of the Army for Manpower and Reserve Affairs to revise Army Regulation 600-8-104, Military Personnel Information Management/Records, to require that the Army's Human Resources Command periodically review and confirm that service member Official Military Personnel File records in iPERMS or other master personnel record systems are consistent and complete to support annual financial audit requirements.

DoD RESPONSE: Concur. ECD: June 30, 2013

- 2 -

Appendix III: GAO Contact and Staff Acknowledgments

GAO Contact	Asif A. Khan, (202) 512-9869 or khana@gao.gov
Staff Acknowledgments	In addition to the contact named above, Gayle L. Fischer, Assistant Director; Carl S. Barden; Tulsi Bhojwani; Frederick T. Evans; Lauren S. Fassler; Wilfred B. Holloway; Sabur O. Ibrahim; John J. Lopez; Julia C. Matta, Assistant General Counsel; Sheila D. M. Miller, Auditor in Charge; Margaret A. Mills; Heather L. Rasmussen; Ramon J. Rodriguez; James J. Ungvarsky; and Matthew P. Zaun made key contributions to this report.

GAO's Mission	The Government Accountability Office, the audit, evaluation, and investigative arm of Congress, exists to support Congress in meeting its constitutional responsibilities and to help improve the performance and accountability of the federal government for the American people. GAO examines the use of public funds; evaluates federal programs and policies; and provides analyses, recommendations, and other assistance to help Congress make informed oversight, policy, and funding decisions. GAO's commitment to good government is reflected in its core values of accountability, integrity, and reliability.
Obtaining Copies of GAO Reports and Testimony	The fastest and easiest way to obtain copies of GAO documents at no cost is through GAO's website (www.gao.gov). Each weekday afternoon, GAO posts on its website newly released reports, testimony, and correspondence. To have GAO e-mail you a list of newly posted products, go to www.gao.gov and select "E-mail Updates."
Order by Phone	The price of each GAO publication reflects GAO's actual cost of production and distribution and depends on the number of pages in the publication and whether the publication is printed in color or black and white. Pricing and ordering information is posted on GAO's website, http://www.gao.gov/ordering.htm.
	Place orders by calling (202) 512-6000, toll free (866) 801-7077, or TDD (202) 512-2537.
	Orders may be paid for using American Express, Discover Card, MasterCard, Visa, check, or money order. Call for additional information.
Connect with GAO	Connect with GAO on Facebook, Flickr, Twitter, and YouTube. Subscribe to our RSS Feeds or E-mail Updates. Listen to our Podcasts. Visit GAO on the web at www.gao.gov.
To Report Fraud, Waste, and Abuse in Federal Programs	Contact: Website: www.gao.gov/fraudnet/fraudnet.htm E-mail: fraudnet@gao.gov Automated answering system: (800) 424-5454 or (202) 512-7470
Congressional Relations	Katherine Siggerud, Managing Director, siggerudk@gao.gov, (202) 512-4400, U.S. Government Accountability Office, 441 G Street NW, Room 7125, Washington, DC 20548
Public Affairs	Chuck Young, Managing Director, youngc1@gao.gov, (202) 512-4800 U.S. Government Accountability Office, 441 G Street NW, Room 7149 Washington, DC 20548

Please Print on Recycled Paper.

www.ingramcontent.com/pod-product-compliance
Lightning Source LLC
Chambersburg PA
CBHW080921290526
45795CB00007BA/2613